The C
Who

Stories by
DOROTHY EDWARDS

Illustrated by Thelma Lambert

'The Old Man Who Sneezed',
'The Wicked Birds and
The Cherry Tree',
'The Miserable Mouse',
and many others.
Children will soon find
their own favourites
from these charming stories
with that special Dorothy Edwards touch.

The Old Man Who Sneezed

Dorothy Edwards

A Magnet Book

First published 1983 by Methuen Children's Books Ltd
Magnet paperback edition published 1985
by Methuen Children's Books Ltd
11 New Fetter Lane, London EC4P 4EE

Printed in Great Britain
by Richard Clay (The Chaucer Press) Ltd, Bungay, Suffolk
ISBN 0 416 51920 2

With the exception of *The Old Man Who Sneezed*,
the stories in this collection were
previously published in the following volumes:
More Naughty Little Sister Stories and Some Others,
Methuen & Co Ltd, 1957; *Listen, Listen*, BBC, 1970;
A Storychair Book, Transworld Publishers, 1971;
Listen With Mother Stories, BBC, 1972;
The Read-To-Me Story Book, Methuen, 1974;
Stories for Bedtime, Collins, 1975;
The Read-Me-Another Story Book, Methuen, 1976;
Once, Twice, Thrice Upon a Time, Lutterworth, 1976

Contents

The old man who sneezed

There was an old man who sneezed and sneezed
He sneezed and sneezed: A-A-TISHOO!
AH-AH-AH-AH-
AH-AH-AH-AH-
TISH-OOO!
Just like that!
He sneezed till his eyes were wet.
He sneezed till his ears popped.
He sneezed so long and he sneezed so loud:
He sneezed till his nose blew off
AH-AH-TISHOO.

The old man's nose blew off and away
It shot out of the door,
Into the street and over the road.
It just missed a bus.
It just missed a car.

It only just missed a lorry!
Across the road went that old man's nose.
Over a pavement,
Through a front-door,
Down a passage,

And right into a kitchen where a dear old lady was eating her breakfast, and it fell into that old lady's cornflakes!
There it lay, the old man's nose, all among the crispy yellow cornflakes!
It made the old lady jump.
"Dear me, dear me," the old lady said.
"How did that nose get there?"
And she put on her glasses and looked again:
"What a *big* nose! What a *red* nose. It looks just like the nose that belongs to the old man over the road," that old lady said.
Now the old man who sneezed was very upset when his nose blew away.

He wanted to sneeze again.
"I can't sneeze without my nose," he said.
So he began to chase it.
He ran out of the door into the street, but *he* was careful.
He let a bus go by.
He let a car go by.
He let a lorry go by.
He looked both ways and didn't try to cross the road until it was absolutely clear, even though he wanted to sneeze very badly.
He managed to AH-
He could AH-AH
But he really couldn't Tishoo!
But when the road was safe he ran over the road to the old lady's house.
But he didn't run through her front door.
He was a very polite old man.
Even though he wanted to sneeze he wouldn't go in without being asked.
Because he was polite he waited on the old lady's step.
He knocked on the old lady's door.
He rang the old lady's bell.
He rattled the old lady's letter-box.
"Have you got my nose in there?" he called.
"Come in, come in," said the dear old lady.
"I've got your nose here – it's perfectly safe.
It fell in my cornflakes and wasn't hurt a bit.
I'll put it back on for you if you like," the old lady said.
So the old man went into the old lady's kitchen and

she put his nose back on for him.
"There!" she said. "That won't come off in a hurry. But how did you come to lose it?"
"I sneezed it off," the old man said.
"And I very much want to sneeze again, only I'm afraid it will blow off. I have very strong sneezes," the old man said.
"Yes my dear," said the old lady. "I see what you did – You forgot to be polite.
You were polite about not coming into my house without knocking first, but you weren't polite about sneezing.
YOU DIDN'T USE A HANDKERCHIEF.
No wonder your nose blew off."
She went to her cupboard and got him three paper ones.
"Hold those to your nose when you sneeze," she said.
"You'll be as right as rain."
So the old man held the three paper handkerchiefs to his nose.
Then he sneezed and sneezed:
"A-A-TISHOO!
AH-AH, AH-AH,
AH-AH, AH-AH,
TISHOO!"
He sneezed so loud he made the old lady jump.
He sneezed so loud that her door-bell rang by itself.
Her knocker knocked by itself,
Her letterbox rattled by itself.
All the buses in the road stopped.
The cars stopped.

The lorries stopped.
"AH-AH, AH-AH,
AH-AH, AH-AH,
TISH-ISH-ISH-ISH-ISHOO!"
That was the biggest sneeze of all!
But because he held the handkerchiefs close to his face the old man's nose stayed on.
Even though he sneezed again:
"ATISHOO, ATISHOO."
And then again (not so loud) "ah-tishoo."
Then quieter still: "ah-tishoo."
And then so quiet only he could hear it: "........!"
But his nose stayed where it belonged.
And it never came off again, for he always remem-

bered to be polite and to look for a handkerchief before he sneezed:

"AH-AH-AH-AH-TISHOO!"

Now the old lady can eat her breakfast, and the traffic can go up and down the road without anyone having to worry about that old man's nose!

Joey and Uncle Ron

Little Joey Tomkins has three big brothers and three big sisters who all go to school. In school-time they are away all day, but in the holidays they are always in and out of the house. Joey likes holiday times because then his big brothers and sisters play with him and sometimes they take him out for walks.

But one day in the holidays Joey's big brothers and sisters all went out for the day and left him behind with his mother, and he was very, very cross.

He shouted and cried and banged because they had gone out without him, but his mother said: "It's no good being naughty, Joey. They've gone now, and they won't be home till tea-time!"

She said: "You don't make a fuss like this when they go to school. So why don't you pretend it's an ordinary school-time day and do the things you do when you haven't got the others at home to play with you?"

So Joey stopped crying.

"Can you remember all the things you do when they are at school?" his mother asked him.

And Joey thought, and remembered something right away!

He remembered that every morning on the days when the big children were at school he liked to go upstairs and look out of the front bedroom window and watch all the vans come down the road. So he went straight upstairs to the front bedroom and stood on his special chair by the window and looked out at the road, and pretended it wasn't a holiday day at all.

He pulled the curtain back a little bit, and looked, and – yes! There was something to see already! It was the coalman's big black lorry – and there were Nobby and Bert, the two jolly coalmen, lifting the heavy black coal-bags and carrying them round to the back of the lady-over-the-road's house!

"If it had been an ordinary holiday day I wouldn't have seen them at all," said Joey.

He remembered to listen hard and there! *Rumble-rumble*, THUMP! *Rumble-rumble* THUMP! That was the coal going into the lady-over-the-road's coal bunker! Joey knew that noise very well!

Then after that the baker's green van came down

the road. Joey pressed his nose hard against the glass. Yes! There was the baker with the same white apron and the same yellow basket and the same cigarette behind his ear. When he came to Joey's gate he looked up and waved – just as he always waved on school-days, and Joey waved back.

Then the greengrocery van came along, with all the fruit and vegetables on top and the ladies in the road went out and bought potatoes and things just as *they* always did, and while they were still buying, the post-man's red parcels van went down the road and stopped at the house by the lamp-post.

And now Joey began to get very interested. He

listened very hard for *jingle-jangle*! *clitter-clatter*! Now it was the time for Joey to jump off his chair and run downstairs as he always did on school-days. "It's Uncle Ron! It's Uncle Ron!" he shouted.

So it was. It was Uncle Ron – and it was the milkman too! For Uncle Ron, who was Joey's mother's big brother, was the very milkman who came to all the houses in their street.

Uncle Ron was very surprised to see there was only Joey at home today.

"I suppose you don't know what to do with yourself," he said.

"I'm pretending it's a school-day," said Joey, and Uncle Ron said that was a very good idea.

When Uncle Ron's van had gone jingle-jangling away, Joey remembered something else: "We go down to the shops now, don't we?" he said, because of course on school-days there were no big children to do the shopping.

"Goodness, yes, so we do!" said his mother. And she took her shopping basket from the kitchen table and the key from the back door, and off they went to the shops.

Away down the road and round the corner was the place where the big flats were, and they had just got there when they saw, outside the big doorway, Uncle Ron's milk-van. And there was Uncle Ron himself with two big wire baskets full of bottles of milk.

And just as Joey was saying, "Hello" all over again to Uncle Ron, his mother said, "Oh dear! I thought I'd do something silly – I've left my purse at home!

We'll have to walk all the way back, Joey!"

But Uncle Ron said, "You don't have to take him all the way back. Let him stay with me. He can pretend to be a milkman, as this is a pretending day. He can help me deliver some of the milk until you get back."

Joey thought this was a lovely idea, so, while his mother went back home to get her purse, he went into the flats with Uncle Ron.

There was a lift in the flats – just like the lifts Joey had been in with his mother when they went to the big shops! It was standing waiting and empty with the door open all ready, so Uncle Ron and Joey went straight inside, and, after he had put his baskets of milk on the lift floor, Uncle Ron pressed a button and the lift went up, up, up, up, and UP. And stopped.

Then the lift door opened and Joey and Uncle Ron and the baskets of milk all came out, and there they were up at the very top of the flats!

There was a long passage with windows all down one side and doors all down the other side. All the doors were white, but every door had a little doorstep and every little doorstep had been painted a different colour. It was very pretty.

And on every doorstep were empty milk bottles.

"Come on, Milkman," said Uncle Ron, "you pick up the empty ones and I'll put down the full ones."

"All right, Milkman," said Joey and off they went down the long passage. Soon there were bottles full of white milk on all those coloured doorsteps and Uncle Ron's baskets were packed with empty bottles.

"Right-o, Milkman," said Uncle Ron. "Back to the van then!" And down in the lift they went, and out to the van for more full bottles. Then up in the lift they went again to more pretty doorsteps and more empty bottles.

"My word, you're a great help, Joey," said Uncle Ron. "You're so quick! I could do with a mate like you every day."

Then down they went again, and this time, there was Joey's mother waiting for them.

"Come on Joey, we've shopping to do," she said.

"Goodbye Joey-lad," said Uncle Ron. "Thanks for your help. You pretended to be a very good milkman."

And as Joey went off down to the shops with his mother he thought, "I really am having a *very* nice day!"

The wicked birds and the wild cherry-tree

Once upon a time there was a lady who had seven hungry children.

This lady had a wild cherry-tree growing by her front gate.

Every year this tree was covered with cherries.

First they were green and too hard to bite.

Then they were red and too sour to eat.

But THEN they were soft and black.

When they were soft and black, they were ripe and ready to eat – ready to make into pies and jam.

The lady's seven hungry children longed for wild-

cherry pie and wild-cherry jam.

But they never got any, for every year as soon as the tree was covered with cherries the wicked birds came.

They sat on the lady's fence and fidgeted their wings and watched.

If the cherries were hard and green the wicked birds flew up and away into the sky to spy out something else to eat.

If the cherries were red and too sour they prodded each other with their beaks and clattered their wings and flew round and round the tree before they flew up and away into the sky to spy out something else to eat.

But as soon as the cherries were ripe and black, as

soon as they saw the ripe, black fruit, in they flew:

Peck, peck, peck.

In they flew: peck, peck, peck.

In they flew again, peck, peck, peck, till their beaks were full of cherry juice and the cherry-stones fell to the ground.

Plop, plop, plop.

Every day the lady went out with her basket to see if there were any ripe cherries.

All she got was plop, plop, plop as the cherry-stones fell on her head.

And when she looked up, there were the wicked birds going peck, peck, peck.

Peck, peck, peck, at the ripe black cherries.

And the cherry-stones fell, plop, plop, plop!

"Oh dear," said the lady. "What can I do? Children, what can I do about those wicked birds? As soon as the cherries turn black, they peck, peck, peck them all up."

She said: "You'll never get your wild black-cherry pies and your wild black-cherry jam if the birds eat all the cherries up."

And she began to cry.

But her seven hungry children said, "Don't worry, Mum. We'll scare them away. WE WILL THINK OF SOMETHING."

And they did.

When they had thought, those children went round all the streets and knocked at all the doors and asked people to give them their old empty paper bags.

People turned out their drawers and cupboards, and shook out their waste-paper baskets, and soon there was a great pile of paper bags under the wild cherry-tree.

Next day, as soon as they had eaten their breakfasts, those seven children waited under the cherry-tree.

Presently the wicked birds came and sat on the fence and watched. Then they began to fly round the tree looking for the ripe cherries.

When the birds did that, the biggest child blew up one of the paper bags and then he popped it.

POP! – like that.

And the wicked birds screeched with fright, and clawed at the air and flew away.

Presently they flew back again, and the next child had a blown-up bag all ready, and he popped *his* bag:

Pop!

And the wicked birds screeched with fright, and clawed at the air and flew away.

And every time the birds came back, a child popped a bag: POP!

And after a while the children got quite clever and popped three bags, one after the other:

POP! POP! POP!

At last each child took a bag, and blew it up and they all popped the bags at the same time and the POP was so loud, it frightened all the wicked birds away and they never came back again.

By night-time every cherry on that tree was ripe.

The tree was covered with ripe, juicy, black fruit.

So the lady fetched a lot of baskets and a long ladder, and she gave each child an electric torch, and they climbed about the branches and picked every single cherry by torchlight!

Pick, pick, pick, went their fingers.

Pick, pick, pick.

They shone their torches, saw the fruit, then:

Pick, pick, pick.

And there were so many cherries the lady made many, many pies and pots and pots and pots of wild-cherry jam after all!

The wicked birds went, Peck, peck, peck.
The cherry-stones fell, Plop, plop, plop.
The paper bags went, Pop, pop, pop,
And the children's fingers went, Pick, pick, pick!

"M-m-m!"

There is a little girl called Olivia whose Nanni in Switzerland often sends her presents through the post. Sometimes her Nanni sends her covers for her bed, or new woollen cardigans or spicy biscuits cut into shapes. There is always something nice and interesting in Olivia's Swiss Nanni's parcels.

One day the postman brought a long white box with a picture of white flowers on the lid.

Olivia's Mummy undid the string that was around the box, and put her nose to the crack under the lid and said:

"M-m-m! Smell, Olivia! M-m-m!"

And Olivia put *her* nose to the crack under the box-lid and sniffed and said, "M-m-m!" too.

Because there was such a beautiful, *beautiful* scented smell coming out of that box.

Olivia's Mummy took the lid right off the box, and there inside were two bunches of beautiful little white spring-flowers with wet newspaper packed round them to keep them cool. Some of the flowers looked a little bit crumpled, but Olivia's Mummy got two big vases and filled them with water and put the flowers in the water, and very, very soon the crumples were smoothed away and the little white flowers spread out

their petals more and more until the whole place was filled with their special Swiss scent.

"M-m-m!" said Olivia's Daddy when he came home from work.

"M-m-m!" said all the people who happened to come up the stairs and walk by the door of the flat which was Olivia's home. "What a *gorgeous* scent – what is it?"

"It's the 'narcisses' from Switzerland," said Olivia's Mummy. "They grow wild in the fields near the house where my mother lives. I used to help her pick them when I was a little girl."

"I'd like to help Nanni pick 'narcisses'," said Olivia.

"You will one day," her Mummy said. "One day you'll visit Nanni in springtime and you will do just that."

And she did, too! And when she'd picked a big bunch of "narcisses" all by herself, her Swiss Nanni fetched her camera and took a beautiful picture of Olivia in her yellow mac with the ladybirds and beetles pattern on it and her yellow boots with the strings round the top to keep them up with, and she sent it to Olivia's English Granny.

And Olivia's English Granny liked it so much that she put it on the table by her window so that everyone could see what a nice little half-Swiss grand-daughter she had.

And do you know what Olivia is doing in that picture? She has her nose very near the flowers and although you can't hear her of course, you've only got to look at her to know she's saying "M-m-m!"

Charlie and the bright moon

There was once a little boy called Charlie who had four big noisy brothers who went to school and a big bouncy sister who went to work and a tiny baby sister who was either smiling or fast asleep, and a very kind Mum and Dad. They all lived together in a little old house in the country.

Charlie's big bouncy sister only worked for half a day on Wednesday, so on Wednesday afternoons, if the weather was fine she would say, "Oh Mum, stop working, do!"

She'd say: "You sit down and rest until Dad and

the boys come home, and I'll take Charlie and Baby down to see our Gran."

And she'd hustle and bustle and bounce about and in no time at all they'd be off, the pram bouncing and bumping, the baby smiling and blinking, and Charlie hopping and skipping. Away and away down the country lanes to the house in the village where their Gran lived.

It was quite a long way to their Gran's house, and now and again when Charlie's legs got slow, Big Sister would lift him up and make him a seat at the bottom of the pram, so that he could ride comfortably all the way. Charlie liked *that*. He liked to feel Baby Sister's little warm feet kicking against his knees while the pram hurry-hurried and his big sister bounced behind him as she pushed the pram along.

Now, as a rule Big Sister liked to get them home before darkness came. That was all right in summer time, but when winter comes darkness starts very early. So, one Wednesday evening when they left their Gran's house and set off for home it was beginning to get dark.

Charlie couldn't remember having been out at this time in the evening before, and he looked about him as Big Sister pushed the pram up the hill. Everything was very quiet and grey, and the houses in the village looked as if they were fast asleep.

When they got to the top of the hill where the post-office shop was, the shop window suddenly lit up. Charlie was so surprised he said "Oh" out loud. Then a window in a house across the road lit up, and he said "Oh" again.

"It's lighting-up time," Big Sister said. "Look Charlie, more lights!"

And she turned the pram round a bit and pointed, and lights twinkled up one by one all down the hill as the street-lamps lit up.

"Lights," Charlie said to his baby sister. "Pretty lights." But Baby was fast asleep.

All the way through the village Charlie saw more and more lights coming out of windows; red lights behind red curtains, green lights behind green curtains, yellow lights behind yellow curtains.

Charlie said: "Red! Green! Yellow!" as they went by.

But they soon left the village and the lights behind them, and were out on the dark country lanes going bumpetty-bump home.

"Lights all gone," Charlie said to Baby Sister, but she was sound asleep now under the pram-hood.

"What about that light, though?" asked his big sister, and she leaned over and pointed. Charlie saw, high above the pram-hood, high above the dark trees in front of them, a great big, shining, bright-white light.

A round, round, staring, smiling light in the sky in front of them. It was so bright it lit up all the roadway and the trees and the hedges!

But it didn't stay still for them to walk past it as they had walked past the village lights. As fast as Big Sister pushed, that round light was always just in front of them. Sometimes it nearly hid itself behind little clouds, sometimes it came out strong and bright.

"Chase it, chase it," Charlie said, and his bouncy sister laughed and hurried the pram along faster yet. "Chase it," said Charlie again.

"It's the moon, the moon," said Big Sister. "It won't stop for us."

But it *did* stop after all. It stopped right over the roof of their very own home. It stood still in the sky and it shone all over the house and the garden and the hedges and fields. "Here you are, home at last," it seemed to say.

Charlie talked and talked when his sister got him ready for bed. He talked louder than his big noisy brothers. He talked about the lights he had seen: the

window lights and the street lights and the light of the moon. "We chased it all the way home," he said.

When Charlie was in bed, Big Sister pulled back the window curtains. There was the big moon right outside, all tangled up among the branches of an apple tree as if it couldn't get away.

"Goodnight, goodnight moon," Charlie said, and he fell asleep with the big moon shining at him through his bedroom window.

The miserable mouse

There was once a mouse who lived in a house with an old lady and an old gentleman. It wasn't a happy mouse, because it hadn't any friends. It wanted friends very much, it specially wanted to be friends with the old lady and gentleman it lived with, but it was no good.

They didn't like mice.

If the old lady even caught a glimpse of it, she would shriek and jump on her chair, and that isn't the way to behave to a lonely mouse who wants to be friends, is it?

As for the old gentleman, he had just to see the merest flicker of a mousy whisker, and he would jump up with a roar and bang, bang, bang on the floor in such a way that he made it very clear he didn't want to be friendly either!

It was *such* a pity. It was such a nice brown clean beady-eyed mouse, with *such* a whippy tail, and such a friendly nature!

"I can't abide mousies," the old lady said, "creeping, stealing creatures is mousies! Always a-eating and a-nibbling they be."

That wasn't true of *this* mouse for a start. Of course, he had to eat – everyone has to do that. But mousie only took crumbs and bits from the floor that no one wanted anyway. He never even dreamed of stealing the large pieces of cheese he saw on the mousetrap that the old people left on the kitchen floor!

"One mouse means many mice," the old gentleman said. "If we don't rid ourselves of this one, we'll be overrun!"

Which just showed that the old gentleman didn't know much about it. Our mouse was the only one in that house, and it takes two mice to be a father and a mother and make lots of little baby mice, doesn't it?

No, it was very dull for our mouse to be a mouse-on-his-own, especially as he knew the old people didn't like him. However, he thought he would be *very patient* and try to win them round. In the meantime, he made a little hole in the wainscot, which he used like a window, so that he could see the old people, although they couldn't see him. It was very interesting too. The old lady did lots of darning and mending, and the old gentleman looked at the television in the evening. Mousie couldn't understand this at all.

Up would go the old lady's arm with a thread of wool hanging from it, and the needle flashed and the thimble glittered in the lamplight. It was very hard for mousie to make out what she was doing. For mice don't wear the sort of clothes that need mending!

And as for the old gentleman and his box of jumping lights! Well, if they'd only be friendly they would soon find that Mouse was more interesting than that old thing. Mouse could whisk for them and frisk for them, and lick his paws and jump for them. Oh, if only they would *take* to him! So Mouse was lonely. And it might have gone on like that forever. Mouse might even have gone back to live with his relations, if it hadn't been for a careless man in a television studio, who fell over a long wire and stopped all the television sets in all the people's houses from showing the programme the old gentleman was looking at.

It was a cowboy film, and the nasty man in the film was just creeping up behind the good nice cowboy when the picture disappeared, so the old gentleman was very cross.

Because he *was* cross, he jumped up quickly, and that made the old lady prick her finger with her darning needle. At the same time, she dropped her thimble, and it rolled across the floor, and dropped right through the hole that was the mouse's front door. The clumsy television man soon put the film back again, so that the old gentleman could see the nice cowboys and nasty men fighting, but the poor old lady was quite lost without her thimble – she couldn't finish her mending!

She hunted and hunted for it, but she couldn't find it. She sighed and fidgeted so much that she upset the old gentleman. How could he look at cowboys, when the old lady was crawling round his chair? So he got up and helped her.

But oh dear, the thimble was lost!

"Oh deary me!" said the old lady. "Now I can't finish my mending. I'm lost without my mending, that I be." And she sat down in her chair and sighed and sighed.

And that was the mouse's chance!

Quick as a flash, he darted out of his hole and into the room. He came with a jingle-jingle noise and they both saw him at once. He was jingle-jingling because he was balancing that thimble on his right-hand front whisker, and as it jiggled about it jangled like a little bell. The little mouse stood quite still at the old lady's feet, and sat himself up just like a little begging dog, and twiddled his whisker with the thimble on it again and again.

"Bless the little creature," said the old lady. "It's brought me thimble, so 'tas. The pretty dear then! Look, Dad, did you ever?"

The old gentleman stared and stared. "W-e-ll I'll be blowed," he said.

The old lady stooped down, and gently, gently she

took the thimble from Mousie's whisker, and put it back onto her finger.

"Don't go Mousie," she said. "I'm just going to get our evening cocoa and biscuits. You might as well stay and have a bite to eat with us."

And she went off to the kitchen at once, and very soon she came back, not only with the cocoa and biscuits, but a whole saucerful of tasty bits from the larder.

The mouse ate them very daintily, and washed his whiskers afterwards to show that he was a clean, good-mannered creature.

"When you've finished that-there blow-out," said

the old gentleman, "you can come and watch the tallyvision along o'me."

And that was just what the mouse wanted. At last he had a chance to see properly what it was that the old man watched in the evening.

He climbed happily onto the old gentleman's knee, and sat twirling his whiskers and looking at the cowboys, and although he couldn't make head or tail of it, he was happy as happy. From time to time the old lady looked across and smiled at him, and from time to time the old gentleman stroked his soft grey fur.

Now, he was more than a friend. He was one of the family!

The biggest one of all

There was once a big strong father called Mr Brown and a big smiling mother called Mrs Brown.

They had a big bouncing girl called Brenda Brown
A big brave boy called Bertie Brown
A not-quite-so-big boy called Bobby Brown
And a not-nearly-so-big girl called Barbara Brown
And a tiny tiny not-big-at-all boy called Baby Bill: Baby Billy Brown.

And they all lived in a not-very-big house in a not-very-long street in a not-very-large town.

Now everybody in the Brown family had jobs to do.

Father Brown worked in a factory
Mother Brown worked in the house
Brenda Brown worked in a shop
Bertie Brown worked hard at school
Bobby Brown worked *very* hard at school

Barbara Brown worked hard making birthday presents for all the other Browns, and Baby Billy worked hard to keep everybody happy by being a good boy.

One day, when all the family were sitting round the table eating their breakfast, Baby Billy said, "Why is Barbara bigger than me, and Bobby bigger than Barbara, and Bertie bigger than Bobby, and Brenda bigger than Bertie and Mother bigger than Brenda and Father biggest of all? Why aren't we all the same size, I wonder?"

Then all the rest of the Brown family laughed. But their mother said, "That's a good question Billy, and here is the answer:

"Barbara is bigger than you because she is older than you.

Bobby is bigger than Barbara because he is older than her.

Bertie is bigger than Bobby because he's older than Bobby.

And Brenda is bigger than Bertie because she is older than Bertie."

And Billy said, "I see; and you are older than Brenda, so you are bigger than she is, and Father is older than you so he is bigger than you are!"

And everyone laughed.

And after that Billy thought a lot about being big and being old.

Well now! Another morning when the Browns were all eating their breakfast eggs and drinking their breakfast cups of tea and Billy was drinking milk, the postman brought a letter.

He brought a letter for Mother Brown.

She asked Brenda to look after the teapot for her while she opened it and read it. When she'd read it right through she said, "Good."

Then she gave it to Father Brown to read and he said, "Ha-ha!" and all the Brown children stopped eating and drinking and looked at each other.

Mother Brown said, "Now we *have* got a piece of news."

And all the family leaned forward to hear, even Father Brown, who knew what the news was.

Mother Brown said, "My dear old great-great grandad is coming to live with us. He won't be living with my Auntie Min any more because she is going over the sea to live with Cousin Tom in Canada. That dear old man is coming to live with us. Won't that be nice?"

And all the Browns but Billy said, "Yes" because they knew all about their mother's dear old great-great grandad and they started to tell each other what a dear old man he was.

When Billy heard them say this he said "Yes" too.

"He's a very old, old, old, old man," Mother Brown said, "so we shall have to take great care of him."

And the big Brown children said, "Of course!"

But Baby Billy asked a question. He said, "Where will he sleep though?" Because as you know the house where the Brown family lived wasn't very big.

"Ah!" said Mother Brown. "I thought someone would ask me that! Well now," she said, "we will clear out the attic and you boys can have it for your bedroom. It's very big and there will be lots of room for all your things and great-great grandad can have your room."

Bertie Brown and Bobby Brown cheered when they heard this. They liked to think of themselves living high up under the roof of the house in the big, big attic, and Baby Billy cheered too because they did.

And so, next day Mother Brown and Brenda Brown cleared out the attic. They brushed the walls and washed the floor and cleaned the windows and hung curtains.

Father Brown burned rubbish and put up shelves and tidied things away in cupboards.

Bertie Brown and Bobby Brown carried up their beds and bedding and Baby Billy's cot-bed and bedding, the chairs and the table, and all their books and toys. Then they helped Father Brown to carry up the chest of drawers. Baby Billy carried his toys upstairs himself.

While they were working, Barbara Brown got lunch ready for them, and, when they had eaten that, they all went upstairs to the boys' old room and made it comfortable and ready for the dear old great-great grandad.

When it was finished the room looked very nice. There was a neat little bed, a nice little armchair, a new table, a wardrobe, a chest of drawers, and some pretty new curtains with green and red leaves on them.

Father Brown and Mother Brown and Brenda Brown and Bertie Brown and Bobby Brown and Barbara Brown were *very* pleased when they looked round that fresh tidy room and saw how nice it looked.

But Baby Billy wasn't pleased. He looked at that neat little bed, and that nice little armchair and he shook his head. He didn't say anything, he shook his head!

And, when Father Brown and Bertie Brown had gone to the station to meet the dear old man, and all the big Brown children were looking out of the front window to see the taxi with Father Brown and Bertie Brown and great-great grandad in it come, Billy went upstairs and looked at that room all over again.

Mother Brown went upstairs to see what had happened to him. There he was, shaking his head and saying, "Oh dear!"

"What's wrong, Billy?" she asked.

"The boys are older than me and they have got bigger beds than I've got, and you and father have got a very big bed. That old, old, old, old, old great grandad must be a very big man. He will want a very big bed and a very big chair, because he is much older than Daddy!"

Then Mother Brown smiled. "Oh Billy," she said, "there's big and bigger and old and older! You'll learn when you're a bigger boy yourself."

Just then the taxi came and all the family went out onto the pavement to say "Welcome" to their mother's great-great grandfather. And Billy saw – not a great big, giant man who would need a big, big, giant bed, but a tiny, tiny, little bendy wrinkly old, old smiling man who could almost have slept in Billy's own cot-bed, he was so very small.

"Why," said Billy. "You aren't big at all. I thought you would be very big because you are so old."

And the dear old man said, "When you get to my age you start growing down, Billy!"

And all the Brown Family laughed. So that was all right.

The dog who frightened the sea

There was once a corgi-dog called Peter who lived with a boy and girl called Jane and Frank.

One day they all went to the seaside for a holiday. They stayed in a white house that was very near the sea. There were three white steps going up to the front door, and inside the front door was a slippery hall with rugs on it. When they arrived, Peter ran straight up those steps and through that door, sent the rugs flying, and slipped and slithered right to the foot of the stairs.

"What do they want to come to a slidy place like this for?" he grumbled.

He grumbled when they went down on to the beach. He could see that Jane and Frank thought it was a lovely place, but he couldn't understand why. It was sandy and stony and there was all that nasty salty moving water!

"I wish we had stayed in our own home," he said to himself. "I like our house where the floors aren't slidy, and the garden where there is nice brown earth and green grass and where the water lives in taps."

But Jane and Frank only laughed at him.

"This sand-stuff won't even make me properly dirty," he grumbled, and he rolled about in it to try, and Jane and Frank laughed more than ever.

So he settled himself down with his nose on his front paws and looked hard at the sea.

Soon the children were running along the water's edge, jumping when the little waves rushed at their feet. They watched the coloured seaweed riding in on top of the big waves, and when the sea went back a little they ran in, snatched up the seaweed and ran along the beach with it.

"Come on, Peter Corgi," they said, "come and play!"

"Ah now, that looks like fun," said Peter, and he jumped up and rushed down the beach towards them, and tried to catch the seaweed in their hands. As they ran he bounced along beside them. Now he was happy!

But oh dear! Jane and Frank ran on and on, straight into that dreadful sea! Peter only just stopped himself in time, right on the edge of the water! He stood there and stared at the rushing tumbling waves. He saw those big waves coming in over and over each other and he didn't like them.

"O-O-O-O-" he said out loud.

"Come on, Corgi," said Jane, "it's lovely!"

But Peter didn't move. He stared and stared at that water that wouldn't stay still. He put back his ears and stuck his feet into the wet sand, and made a whiny-piny noise that meant: "Come out! Come out!" But Jane and Frank only laughed and splashed at him, so he turned and ran back to the white house. Up the steps he went, skitter-scatter among the rugs, then up the stairs where he hid himself under Frank's bed.

After that the children tried very hard to make Peter like the sea. Sometimes Frank threw a ball for Peter to bring back to him. Peter would dash across the sand and fetch the ball and bring it back wagging his stumpy tail with the greatest pleasure. But when Frank threw it into the sea and said, "Get it! Good

dog!" he pretended that he didn't know where it had gone, and ran up and down the beach as if he were looking for it among the stones.

When the children went into the sea to bathe he tried to make them come out. He ran along the edge of the sea with the ball in his mouth, and now and again he dropped it, and sat beside it, and looked to see if Jane and Frank were coming out to play with him. When they took no notice he ran along the beach barking at the waves and showing his teeth at them.

"I wish he would come in the water and play with us," the children said.

But their mother said, "Don't worry him, he'll come when he wants to."

So Peter went on not liking the sea. He was very jealous of those big waves that Jane and Frank seemed

to like so much. "Great big fidgety things," he growled.

Then one afternoon a strange thing happened. The children were playing with a little boat and jumping and splashing in the water. It was a nice little boat with white sails and they were so pleased with it they didn't notice an extra big wave come curling over the sea. Peter did though!

He sat up and watched it as it came rolling in, and, as it came "whoosh" it picked up the little boat and flung it on to the sand, and at the same time – "whoosh" – it tumbled Jane and Frank over. How they laughed!

But Peter was very cross! That bad old sea had tumbled his children over! He jumped up barking and barking. He tore straight down the beach, straight

into the waves and BIT THE SEA.

Oh, it did taste nasty! And a piece of slippery seaweed got tangled in his teeth. But he was so cross, he bit and barked and growled and grumbled until another wave came along and tumbled *him* over too.

The children came out of the water and stared at him as he came out and shook himself. He began to make growly noises.

"Why," said Jane, "he's growling at the sea!" And she put her arm round his wet furry neck. "Silly dog!" she said.

"Grrh-rh-rh," said Peter to the sea, and that meant, "I'll bite you again if you don't behave yourself!"

And would you believe it – slowly, slowly the sea began to go away as the little dog ran up and down the beach in front of it! "Woof-woof! Be off," he barked.

The waves still crept in but each wave was a little smaller than the one before. The big waves had gone already. Soon Peter saw the wet sand and the seaweed drying in the sunshine and the new pink shells laid bare on the shore.

"Ah-ha," barked the corgi-dog, wagging his tiny stumpy tail, "it's going because it's frightened of ME."

He was so proud, he stopped being cross. "Woof, woof," he barked, "I'm not afraid of you," and into the sea he ran. He began to swim to and fro, barking and barking.

"It's going away because I told it to. Look Jane and Frank, the sea's afraid of ME!"

The children ran to where their mother was sitting.

"Look, look," they said. "Look at Peter! He doesn't mind the sea now."

"Indeed he doesn't," their mother told them. "I suppose that's because the tide is turning."

But Peter didn't know that. He thought the sea was going because it was afraid of him.

The lost little red toy car

There was once a little red toy car who lived with a little boy called Gerald.

This little red toy car fitted nicely into Gerald's hand, and Gerald and the little car played lots of games together on Gerald's mum's lounge carpet.

Up and down the carpet the little car would go. Under Gerald's hand: up and down.

"I'm taking Mum to the shops," Gerald would say. He would stop the little red toy car by the sideboard. "Here are the shops, Mum; get out and we'll wait for you."

Or he would pretend to be racing it to catch a train, or that it had broken down and wanted mending, and the little toy car would pretend too and be whatever Gerald wanted it to be and do whatever Gerald wanted it to do.

They were very happy.

One day though when Gerald was racing his little red car it went too fast. It shot out from under his hand, over the floorboards and fell down a hole in the hearth where Gerald's dad was putting in a new fireplace. And there it stayed because no-one knew where it had gone to. Gerald's dad finished putting the fireplace in and the poor little red toy car was lost.

Gerald cried a lot, and then he cheered up and forgot all about the little car.

But the little car thought about Gerald and wished he would find him and play with him again. But he never did.

Gerald grew up. First he was a big boy; then he was a bigger boy; then he was a man and then he got married and was a Daddy Gerald with a little boy called Gerald of his own.

One day Daddy Gerald took little Gerald to see his Gran and Grandad. When they got there Grandad was breaking up the fireplace. He was going to put in a gas-fire. Gerald's little boy Gerald watched him.

Suddenly little Gerald said, "What's that red thing down in that hole, Grandad?"

Grandad looked, and put his hand into the hole and there was the little red car! It was dirty but after Grandad rubbed it on his work-apron it was as good as new. Its wheels spun round as they'd always done and it just fitted into little Gerald's hand.

Little Gerald ran the little red toy car up and down his gran's lounge carpet: up and down. And the little car was perfectly happy again.

"I wonder where that car came from?" said Daddy Gerald. "I don't remember seeing it before."

But the little red toy car didn't mind him saying that. In fact, he didn't know that Daddy Gerald had been the little boy he'd played with so long ago. He was just glad to be playing again with a little boy called Gerald!

The invisible pig

Do you know what "invisible" means?

It's what you say when you are talking about something that's there though you can't see it. Like the wind. You can feel the wind, but you can't see it.

The wind is invisible.

Well now, here is a story about an invisible – PIG!

There was once a very nice old lady who lived with her son, who was an artful, greedy boy.

Now this kind old lady was very fond of animals. She was always feeding them:

Milk for the pussy-cat. *Mia-ow.*

Meat for the dog. *Bow-wow.*

Corn for the hens. *Cluck-cluck.*

She couldn't bear to think of poor hungry animals!

And she couldn't bear to think of hungry boys either! She cooked beautiful dinners for her artful greedy boy and she let him have TWO HELPINGS of everything!

Cakes and puddings
Bread and jam
Meat pies
Cornflakes
Eggs and ham

Um-m-m. Two helpings!

But do you know, that artful greedy boy wasn't satisfied! No. He said he wanted *three* helpings. One, two, three. But his nice, kind old mother said, "Oh no my son, three helpings would be rather piggy!" and she wouldn't let him have them.

That artful greedy boy was very cross. He stuck out his lip and he sulked and sulked.

"Piggy," he said. "Piggy indeed! Why, if I were a piggy instead of a boy she'd give me three helpings!"

And then he had an idea.

This is what he did. He went into the garden and built a fancy pigsty. He built it out of an old broken door, some bits of rusty iron and the top of an old table, and he tied it all together with string. Then he put his mother's old macintosh on top for a roof.

It looked terrible; but then he wasn't a tidy boy.

When his mother saw his fancy sty she said: "Good gracious me, what is that con-trap-tion?"

And her boy said, "It's a fancy sty for my piggy."

The nice old lady said, "But you haven't got a piggy!"

And he said, "Haven't I though?" and he went out to the front gate and opened it and called, "Piggy, piggy, piggy," and brought in a *pretending* pig and pretended to put it in the fancy sty. He tied up the sty door with an old shoe-lace because he hadn't any string left.

His mother said: "I didn't see a pig." And he said, "Oh no, it's a special sort of piggy. It's an *invisible* piggy."

He said, "It's a poor invisible piggy that was looking for a home."

His mother said, "Poor thing! What does it eat?"

And he said: "Nothing special. Just the same as we do. It isn't a fussy animal."

So every day after that, when that artful greedy boy had eaten his two helpings of breakfast or dinner or tea, he would go and get two china dishes for his mother to put the rest of the food in. He *said* it was for the invisible piggy.

He would take that nice food out to his fancy pigsty and pretend to call the pig: "Piggy, piggy don't be shy. Come and eat your dinner."

Then this artful greedy boy would go inside his fancy pigsty with his two dishes of food, and when he was safely hidden under the old macintosh roof he gobbled up every bit of the dinner himself!

And while he gobbled he made snorty grunty snuffly piggy-eating noises, in case his kind old mother was listening.

Then he would say, "Good piggy. Good animal!" and take the dishes indoors to be washed up.

That was very naughty.

Ah yes – but his kind old mother wasn't as silly as you think! For one thing, that artful greedy boy began to get very very fat from eating all that extra food. For another thing, she noticed that the invisible pig never made a sound when that greedy boy wasn't around!

So, one day the old lady crept down to the pigsty and peeped between the rusty old bits of iron, and she saw that artful greedy boy eating all the food himself.

But she didn't say anything to him.

She crept back into the house and she chuckled and cackled: "Ha-ha-ha-ha. Hee-hee-hee-hee." And she made a *plan*.

And the next morning when her son got up she said: "Such news, such news, Sonny dear! This morning early, before you woke up, the invisible farmer who had lost your invisible piggy came to collect him. He had been searching everywhere for him, it seems! But he was a grateful man, and said, many *many* thanks for all our kindness."

When she said this the artful greedy boy opened his eyes very wide, and his mouth very wide – but he didn't know what to say. He just sat down at the breakfast table without a word.

The nice old lady came in smiling and smiling and put a plate in front of him. "Eat it up," she said. "It's very tasty!"

BUT THERE WAS NOTHING ON THE PLATE!

That artful greedy boy stared and stared. "There's nothing there *to* eat!" he said.

His mother said, "Oh, I forgot to tell you. It's invisible bacon. That invisible farmer gave it to me, he was so grateful to us for looking after his invisible piggy for him. He has given me some invisible pork chops for your dinner and some invisible ham for your supper. Wasn't that kind of him?"

Then that artful boy knew he had been found out!

He looked at the empty plate with the invisible breakfast. He thought of those empty plates with his invisible dinner and his invisible supper. But he wouldn't give in.

He took up his knife and fork, and pretended to eat his invisible bacon and pretended not to hear his nice old mother laughing and laughing.

So:

This little pig went to market.
This little pig stayed at home
This little pig had roast beef

This little pig had none
And this little piggy was invisible
And his farmer took him home.

Nice white elastic

One day Ruthie's mother made her a pair of new blue knickers. She made them on her sewing-machine.

When Ruthie's mother had finished making the new blue knickers she found that she hadn't any elastic to put in the top, so the next time she went to the shops she popped into the draper's for some.

"A yard of white elastic, please," she said to the draper's lady.

The draper's lady took out a roll of nice white elastic and she measured off a yard. Then she snipped it off with her scissors. A YARD OF NICE WHITE ELASTIC.

The draper's lady rolled it up and put it into a clean white piece of tissue-paper, and fastened the paper with a bright new pin and gave it to Ruthie's mother.

And Ruthie's mother took it home, and because she had to get Ruthie's father's dinner, she didn't put the elastic into her workbasket. No. She put the yard of nice white elastic in the clean white paper with the new bright pin in it onto the kitchen table and forgot all about it.

NOW, Ruthie had a little brother named Charley, and Ruthie's little brother Charley was making a boat. He made the bottom of the boat from a vinegar-bottle cork, and he had found a tenpenny stamp for the sail, but he was looking for something to fasten the sail on with. So he began to search and search and presently he looked in the kitchen, and there, on the table, stuck in the clean white tissue-paper, he saw the bright new pin.

"That's just what I need to fasten my sail," said Charley. And he took the new bright pin out of the tissue-paper and fastened the stamp on to the vinegar-bottle cork with it, and he had a BOAT.

Now, Ruthie's father was tidying up the garden for the winter. He was cutting down all the dry brown plants and making them into a pile for a bonfire.

Close beside the kitchen door there had been a fine yellow hollyhock plant, and Ruthie's father had been very proud of it, because it had grown right up to the bedroom window! Everyone had admired this very tall hollyhock, so when he cut down its dry brown stem, Ruthie's father pulled off some of its round brown seed-cases.

"I will save these for all the people who admired my hollyhock," he thought, "then they can plant them and have hollyhocks just like mine next year!"

Then Ruthie's father thought, "How can I keep the seed-cases safe? If I put them into my pocket as they are, they are sure to pop open and the seeds will get mixed up with all the other things in my pocket. I must find something to put them in."

So Ruthie's father opened the kitchen door, and put his head in, to see if he could find anything to put the seeds in. (He didn't like to come right into the kitchen because of his muddy gardening-boots).

And you know what he saw on the kitchen table. He saw the clean white tissue-paper. And the clean white tissue-paper was just a little bit open, because there wasn't a pin in it any more.

Ruthie's father just managed to stretch his arm far enough to get hold of a corner of the tissue-paper. "This is just what I want!" he said, and as he pulled it towards him the elastic tumbled out on to the kitchen floor. But Ruthie's father didn't notice the elastic – he was so very pleased to have the nice tissue-paper to put his hollyhock seed-cases in.

And that's just what he did. He put them into the

tissue-paper, and he screwed it up tight at the top and put it into his pocket. Then he went out into the garden again, to light his bonfire.

Ruthie had been upstairs helping her mother to dust the bedrooms, but presently she grew tired of dusting, so she went downstairs to see if she could find anything new and nice to play with. *Anything at all.*

She went into the kitchen and there on the floor she saw the nice white elastic – without any paper – without any pin, lying all white and curly. A YARD OF NICE WHITE ELASTIC.

Now, if that elastic had been wrapped up in tissue-paper, Ruthie wouldn't have touched it. If it had been in tissue-paper with a pin in it, she *certainly* wouldn't have THOUGHT of touching it. But there was *no* tissue-paper, and NO pin!

So Ruthie picked up the elastic and pulled it out and let it go, and pulled it out and let it go and heard it say "ping", but she soon got tired of that.

"I know," said Ruthie, "I will take some of this nice white elastic and make garters for my big teddy, his socks are always falling down!"

So Ruthie fetched her big teddy, and she took some scissors from her mother's workbasket. (That was where the elastic really should have been put in the beginning, wasn't it?)

THEN Ruthie measured the elastic round Teddy's right leg, just as her mother sometimes measured elastic round her leg. She snipped it off, and because she wasn't old enough to thread needles and sew, she tied the elastic in a knot, and there was big Teddy's right-

leg garter all made!

Then Ruthie did exactly the same thing for Teddy's left leg – and there was the left-leg garter – ALL MADE.

And there was big Teddy with garters on. Real elastic garters, with knots instead of stitches, and his socks pulled up tight as tight.

Then, oh dear! *There* was Ruthie's mother. *Very cross.*

"Ruthie!" she said, "you meddlesome child. You've cut up the elastic I bought for your new blue knickers. How could you be so naughty?"

And Ruthie said, "Oh, Mother, I found it on the floor. I didn't know you wanted it."

"On the floor?" said her mother. "But when I left it, it was wrapped in tissue-paper with a pin in it!"

Just then Ruthie's daddy put his head round the back door and said, "Tissue-paper? Oh, I took some tissue-paper off the table for my hollyhock seeds. When I picked it up, I didn't notice any elastic. It must have fallen out."

"But," said Ruthie's mother, "there was a pin in the tissue-paper when I left it on the table."

And Ruthie's little brother Charley, who had been sitting on the back door-step thinking about how he would take his little boat to the seaside next year, looked round the bottom of the door and said, "Oh, I took the pin. I wanted a mast for my boat."

And Ruthie said, "I took some of the elastic to make garters for the big teddy-bear, because his socks are always falling down."

"Well I never did!" said Ruthie's mother. "So that is how it happened. Charley took the pin, and Daddy took the paper, and Ruthie took some of the elastic for her teddy's garters!"

Then she picked up the rest of the elastic and she smiled and smiled.

"It's all right after all," she said. "You made your teddy very tight garters, so there is plenty of elastic left for your new blue knickers!"

And she rolled up the piece of nice white elastic and put it straight into her workbasket.

So everything was right again. Ruthie's father had the paper for his hollyhock seeds, Ruthie's big teddy had new garters, and there was plenty of elastic left for her knickers after all.

And as for Ruthie's little brother Charley, he called his boat the *Elastic Queen* because of the pin from the elastic parcel and the Queen's head on the tenpenny stamp sail.

The old lady doll

There was once a little girl called Mary who had three dolls. She had a girl-doll with yellow plaits, a boy-doll dressed like a sailor and a baby girl-doll who could be bathed like a real baby.

"I've got three children," Mary used to say, "I've got three children and my goodness, they keep me busy!"

And they did, too.

She got them up every morning before she had her breakfast and she put them to bed directly after tea each night.

She cooked nice dinners for them on her toy stove and put plaster on their bad places when they fell down and hurt themselves.

On Saturday mornings she did all their washing and on Saturday afternoons she took them for a walk in their pram to visit their relations in the toy-shop window.

Wasn't she a motherly child?

One day, Mary's mother's friend Miss Lamb wrote to say that she was bringing Mary a doll on her very next visit.

Mary was pleased. "I must get ready for her at once," she said.

She made up a special bed in a cardboard box with the mattress and pillows from the dolls' pram and put

a tiny hot-water bottle between the sheets to make sure the bed was aired.

On the day Miss Lamb was expected, Mary put her boy and girl into their chairs and her baby into its high-chair.

"When the new child comes, I shall say, 'Don't be shy, love,' and you must smile and smile," said Mary.

And the girl-doll smiled, and the boy-doll smiled and even the baby-doll smiled, and Mary saw how pleased they were to have a new relation.

The doll came in a shiny wooden box and Miss Lamb lifted off the wooden lid and folded back layers and layers of soft blue paper – and there she was!

"O," said Mary, "O" – like that, round eyes, round mouth, because she was so surprised. "O, it's an *old lady*!"

Miss Lamb laughed and Mary's mother laughed too.

"Yes, she's a very old lady," Miss Lamb said. "She has lived in my family for two hundred years."

"That's a *very* long time," Mary's mother said.

"When the first little girl who had her grew up, she gave her to *her* little girl, and *her* little girl gave her to HER little girl, over and over again.

"My mother got her from her mother, and she gave her to me," Miss Lamb said, and, as I haven't anyone left in my family to give her to, I thought you'd like her. Her name is Miss Beauty."

"OH, I like her very much," said Mary.

And so she did.

But she knew she couldn't be a mother to Miss

Beauty. She was such a very old lady. You couldn't cuddle and pet and smack her like a child doll. "Good gracious no! That would be RUDE," thought Mary.

"Be careful," said Mary's mother, and Mary lifted Miss Beauty from her tissue paper and held her straight in front of her.

Miss Beauty had a brown, brown face because she was so old, but her eyes were wide and bright and her painted lips smiled sweetly. She wore a green-silky dress and a white-silky apron with rosebuds on it. On her head was a funny white cap with a high lace frill in front of it. She had old lace mittens on her brown stitched hands and she carried a tiny fan and a handkerchief.

The silky dress was so old, it had little cracks in it. The lacy cap was yellow and the fan was so frail Miss Lamb said Mary had better not try to open it.

"I should put her back in her box now," said Mother. So they folded Miss Beauty carefully back into her box and the box went to stay on the top of Mary's wardrobe.

Mary put the pillows and the mattress back into the dolls' pram. "Your new relation is very old indeed and mustn't be disturbed," she told the three children dolls.

But Mary often thought about old Miss Beauty, and sometimes her mother took her down for Mary to look at. "Poor old lady," said Mary. "I expect she is very lonely. I would ask her to have tea with my children, but I am sure they would be too much for her, as she's so very old."

Then one day Mother had a good idea.

"There is a museum in London where they have lots of dolls like your old lady," she said. "I wonder if the museum people would like to put her in one of their show-cases, then lots of people could see her, and she wouldn't get spoiled."

Mary thought about that.

Then she said, "Well, she would have lots of other old ladies to talk to I suppose."

So the next time Mary's daddy went to London he took old Miss Beauty to the museum, and the museum people were *very* glad to see her.

"She is the finest old doll we've ever seen," they said.

1782
1867

So, one day Mary went to the museum with her mother.

It's a lovely place full of old dolls' houses and toys and games and drums and skittles and soldiers and oh – I can't tell you what else – you must go for yourself!

And if you do go, you'll see what Mary saw: there, in a big glass showcase were lots and lots of old dolls. Some sitting, on chairs or curly-backed sofas, and some standing.

There were dolls made of leather. Dolls made of wax, wood dolls and rag-dolls, china dolls and pottery dolls – all old ladies, all dressed in old-fashioned clothes.

Some wore feathers, some wore furs and two fine ladies had their own trunks full of clothes.

And among them, sitting sweet and stiff on a comfortable chair sat Mary's old Miss Beauty. Her green skirt was carefully spread out, and her tiny fan had been gently opened.

She was leaning towards another old doll in a tall cap like her own.

"Oh, she's found a friend," said Mary.

"I think she's found a long-lost sister," said Mary's mother.

"There's a card here that says they were both made by the same doll-maker."

"I know what this place really is," said Mary. "It's a dolls' old-ladies' home!"

"That's a nice idea," she said. "Next time I come, I'll bring my three children to visit their very old relations."

And she did too.

Robert goes to fetch a sister

This story is about a little boy called Robert who lived with his father and mother in a little house with a green gate in a village in the country.

Robert had a dog, a cat and a budgie.

He had lots of nice toys too.

But he hadn't anyone to play with. He hadn't any brothers or sisters.

Robert's Dad worked for the village baker. He drove a yellow van and delivered bread and buns and groceries to people's houses.

Everyone liked Robert's Dad, he was such a

pleasant, friendly man. Always smiling and singing.

Sometimes when Robert's Mum was extra busy, his Dad took him on the bread-round with him.

Robert liked this very much.

They sang songs together as they drove down the country lanes.

Robert's Dad would start singing and Robert would join in.

Sometimes as they drove along they would count the telegraph poles and when they got to "ninety-nine, a HUNDRED" Robert's Dad would sing a song that he'd made up himself.

He'd sing:

"*Ninety-nine, a HUNDRED*
"*Ninety-nine, a HUNDRED*
"*Ninety-nine for Robert*
And a HUNDRED for me."

The people in the houses where they left the bread and groceries were always glad to see Robert. In the summertime they would give him glasses of milk or orange squash. In the winter they'd say, "Come in for a moment and warm yourself by the fire and drink a cup of cocoa to help you on your way this cold morning."

And Robert thought that being with his Dad in the yellow van was the loveliest treat in the world.

Now, Robert had been adopted when he was a baby.

ADOPTED. That means that his Mum and Dad couldn't have children of their own. They had wanted

a little boy so much that they had taken Robert to live with them when he was a tiny baby and had made him their very own child.

Robert liked to hear how he had been adopted.

How his Mum and Dad had gone to fetch him from a big house where there were lots of children who hadn't got fathers and mothers.

When Robert had finished his supper and was sitting on his Mum's lap in his red dressing-gown she would tell him all about it.

"I knew just the sort of little boy I wanted," she would say. "So when I went into a room and saw three little baby boys asleep in their cots I knew which one was mine. I went and picked him up at once."

"Who do you think I picked up?" his Mum would ask.

And Robert would laugh and say, "It was *Me*. It was *Me*."

One day Robert's Mum said, "We are such a happy family, Robert, that Dad and I think it would be a nice thing to adopt another little baby to be happy with us. So next week we are going to fetch a little baby sister for you to play with. Would you like to come with us?"

"Oh yes! Oh yes I *would*," Robert said.

All next week he helped to get Baby Sister's things ready. Mum got out Robert's old cot and pram and some of the clothes he had worn when he was a baby and she took him on a bus to the town to buy lots of new things too.

Everyone in the village knew about the new baby and lots of Robert's Dad's customers gave him things to bring home that they thought would be useful for her.

On the Wednesday of the next week the kind baker lent Robert's Dad the van and off they went to fetch the baby sister.

Robert's Mum sat beside Dad in the front, while Robert sat on a stool in the back where the bread-trays usually went. There was a little window behind his mother's head so that he could talk to her quite easily.

And he did talk too. All the way.

At last they came to the big house Robert had heard so much about. It had a big garden round it and big

gates for them to drive through.

It took the van a long time to get through the garden because there were a lot of children playing there, and Robert's Dad had to drive very carefully.

The children were playing with all sort of things: rocking-horses and sand-pits and balls and skipping-ropes, but they all stopped playing when they saw the yellow van and smiled and waved to Robert and his Mum and Dad.

"Is one of them going to be my sister?" Robert asked his Mum.

"No," she said. "The little babies are in a smaller house behind the big one. They are too tiny to play in the garden."

When they got to the smaller house, a lady in a white coat came down the steps to meet them. She took Robert's hand and helped him up the steps in a very friendly way.

She told him she remembered when *he* had been a tiny baby and his Mum and Dad had come for *him*.

They went into a room where there were some babies lying in cots. Most of them were asleep, but one was lying wide awake, smiling and waving her fat little hands.

"Is that one my new sister?" Robert asked.

"Yes," said the lady, "do you like her?"

"I think she's the nicest of all," said Robert.

Then the kind lady wrapped the new little sister in a blanket and Robert's Mum carried her down to the yellow van. She was fast asleep.

This time Robert sat beside his father and his Mum

sat inside on the stool because she thought it might be too draughty for Baby in the front of the van.

But this time Robert didn't count telegraph poles or watch the trees go by.

He knelt on the seat and peeped through the window at his mother and his new baby sister.

Presently his Dad began to sing.

What did he sing?

He sang: "Pat-a-cake, pat-a-cake" and Robert joined in because he knew that was a good song for a baby sister whose Dad was a Bakers' Man.

"*Prick it and nick it and mark it with B,*
And put it in the oven for Baby and Me," sang Robert.

They didn't sing too loudly, for fear of waking the baby, but even so, when they drove through their village many people looked out of their houses and cottages and listened and said:

"There goes the Bakers' Man, and Robert and his Mum, and the new Baby Sister!"